SAILING PAST

For Stefan Kemp

Sailing Past

By Renee M Waite

Illustrations by Keith Waite

SEAFARER BOOKS

1992

First published by Seafarer Books,
10 Malden Road, London NW5

Distributed in the USA by
Sheridan House Inc.
Dobbs Ferry, N.Y. 10522

First published 1992

ISBN 085036 428 0

*Printed and bound in Great Britain by
Biddles Ltd, Guildford & King's Lynn*

This light-hearted anthology reflects the attitudes and practices of a past era. It is a sampling of the many books and magazines offering advice to yachtsmen between the 1850's and 1950's.

It portrays a yachting life vastly different from that of the modern sailor.

From our position in time many of these attitudes and practices may seem highly amusing. The yachtsman reading this book in his well equipped yacht, may either be glad of his comfort and gadgetry, or he may yearn for a return to a simpler age of sailing.

I would like to thank all those who assisted me in the libraries of the Cruising Association; The Royal Harwich Yacht Club; The Royal Norfolk and Suffolk Yacht Club; and The Pin Mill Sailing Club.

Marjorie Carter for her bibliographical and correction work, and all friends who loaned their books.

No man will be a sailor who has contrivance enough to get himself into jail, for being in a ship is being in a jail with the chance of being drowned.

SAMUEL JOHNSON
The Journal of a Tour to the Hebrides, 1786
by James Boswell

Boat for Sale: If you want to buy a boat or offer your boat for sale it is well to know the 'For Sale' sign on a yacht. Nowadays a lettered notice is mostly lashed to the boat, but sometimes one sees the old time-honoured sign – a broom or a bunch of brushwood hoisted to the mast-head. This can be seen from afar off, and is advisable as an addition to the notice-board – which latter is visible only when a person is close to the yacht.

GEOFFREY PROUT
Brown's Pocket Book for Yachtsmen, 1930

I would, I think, as soon advise a man in his choice of a wife as I would in his choice of a ship for they have this much at least in common, that the ideal is hard to find and as diverse as the seekers after it.

ALEC GLANVILLE
Elements of Yacht Sailing and Cruising, 1939

In surveying an old vessel, soft spots can be detected by thrusting a penknife into the wood; or better, with light blows from a hammer. If possible, remove some of the saloon panels, for the space between a vessel's skins is a favourite nest for dry rot.

E. F. KNIGHT
Sailing;
revised and brought up to date by J. Scott Hughes, 1938

Winter work fitting out. Bring home some of the work. If the running gear requires overhaul or renewal, it may be done much more comfortably – always providing the 'O.C House' permits – at home by your fireside on a winter's night, than in a chilly shed. For serving splices, a stout table may be capsized and the rope set up between its legs.

PERCY WOODCOCK
Fitting Out, 1938

The mast has to be tackled in a bo'sun's chair of course on a fine windless day and is inclined to be a sticky, precarious job swinging about with a varnish pot slung to your waist or in a bucket, and requires the co-operation of another to hoist and lower you as you progress. It is almost worth while to have it done for you in these conditions unless you are content to haul yourself upon the throat halliard and quickly rub down with a fat collar of bacon rind. This is quite a good protection for the spar though it lacks the finish of varnish.

TALLY HO
Completing Your Fit Out.
Yachting Monthly and Marine Motor Magazine, 1930

When an owner is unable to claim speed, handiness or beauty for his ship he calls her a magnificent sea boat.

R. D. GRAHAM and J. E. H. TEW
A Manual for Small Yachts, 1946

13

Beware the well-painted and well-varnished yacht for sale: paint and enamel on a "she" afloat can serve the same purpose as paint and enamel on a "she" ashore.

JOHN IRVING
Well Whipped Ropes' Ends
(John Irving and Douglas Service
The Yachtsman's Weekend Book), [1938]

Testing for Strains: Crooks of all sorts, knees, quarterhooks, breast-hooks, running breast hooks, etc. – can generally be tested by gripping with the hand and jerking up and down or to and fro, or by thumping hard, hammerwise, with the clenched hand. When a boat is aground, if she is small enough, her rigidity can be tested by gripping her at the stem and heaving to and fro, abeamwise. If there is give it will be noticed.

GEOFFREY PROUT
Brown's Pocket Book for Yachtsmen, 1930

When practising have an old boat, a safe place like the Crouch, and plenty of room. In a week a learner will be fit to go anywhere, if he has managed his ship without professional assistance during that time.

FRANK COWPER
Sailing Tours: The Coasts of Essex and Suffolk:
The Thames to Aldborough, 1892

Painting the underside of the deck – short of a bathing suit, one's oldest sweater and grey bags are the most suitable wear for this operation, though I have known a man put on his oilskins.

The bottom: Though out of sight most of the time, the bottom should never be out of mind, for its condition, far more than that of the more obvious topsides, will make or mar the performance of the ship, especially in light winds. It should be smoothed down as much as possible, and, again, if bad enough, scraped down to the bare wood. The bottom is usually scraped dry, and the condition of the scraper – the human one, not the tool – will leave much to be desired at the end of a long day. It is advisable to wear a wide brimmed hat with a fine veil or goggles, otherwise you will emulate the performance of a weeping willow.

PERCY WOODCOCK
Fitting Out, 1938

The Refit of *Hawke*, an 1886 (28ft. 4in. overall) boeier.

On the opposite side, hedonistic luxury, appeared a diminutive (4 ft.) bath, round which was evolved, after a week of experimenting, a series of flaps that provided a kitchen table, a wash basin and draining-board, and in which came the plate rack. To supply the bath we installed a small and efficient stove (most elegantly chromium-plated), which, in conjunction with two tanks and a maze of self-designed pipe lines, actually did produce piping hot water in well under the half hour.

The vast open well of the cockpit was made smaller, to accommodate out of harm's way, a 40 gallon tank for water, a 20 ditto for petrol, a 5 ditto for paraffin, and also, last but not least, a baby Electrolux, the yachtsman's joy, one of those marvellous affairs which, by the paradoxical process of lighting a paraffin lamp, ices your water, beer or champagne.

MERLIN MINSHALL
Taking Hawke Across Europe.
Yachting Monthly and Motor Boating Magazine, 1936

The soldier and I had our baths, one after the other, in the cabin, but the parson preferred to have buckets of water poured over him on deck.

A Month's Cruise in 1878
Hunt's Yachting Magazine, 1880

The owner of a yawl sailed to a port some forty miles away and could not make out why she seemed so "tender", i.e. laid over by the wind. However, he made port all right, and after three or four weeks, had the boat brought ashore for a scrub. The news the watermen who scrubbed her gave him was almost unbelievable; his keel had dropped off.

H. H. HEATHER
Sailing for Amateurs, 1910

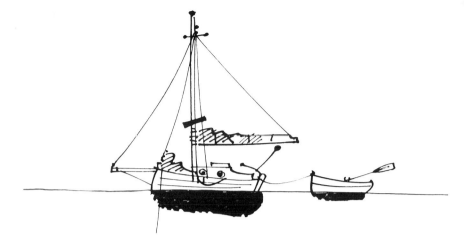

Anchors: Some owners are extremely casual about their ground tackle and seem to think that anything will hold a yacht. When I was at Pin Mill, a small converted ship's boat of about 3 tons was anchored near me. She was manned by three lads of the working class, who had sailed her down from Ipswich, and from the sounds of revelry that came from her cabin it was evident 'a good time was being had by all'. She was riding to a warp that seemed no thicker than an average clothes line and when the tide began to ebb she began to drag her anchor. When informed of the fact, her crew emerged and proceeded to get the anchor. Curious to see what sort of anchor it was that dragged in a flat calm I watched them. When it came to the surface the anchor proved to be the end of an old iron bedstead!

FRANCIS B. COOKE
Cruising Hints, 1948

My advice to all intending yachtsmen is to steer as closely as possible to the law, and it is therefore best to have on board a copy of the Merchant Shipping Act of 1854 with its various amendments. It can be obtained for 3s 6d. and it will be found of great use to the amateur sailor in his dealings with the crew.

TYRELL E. BIDDLE
The Corinthian Yachtsman, or, Hints on Yachting, 1886

Another point I would beg your particular attention to, piratical looking caps and shirt sleeves, with the accompaniment of long clay pipes, do not look nice on a neat well ordered quarterdeck, nor do post prandial orgies accompanied by vocal illustrations of a "Life on the Ocean wave" tend much to modest repute.

"VANDERDECKEN" [William Cooper]
The Yacht Sailor, 1862

One piece of advice. Never allow any approach to undue familiarity upon the part of hands. Also strictly forbid the use of foul and indecent expletives, accustom the crew to regard the after part of the vessel as sacred from such profanity and then you will be spared the mortification of having to apologise to your disgusted and humiliated lady visitors for any laxity in this respect.

TYRELL E. BIDDLE
The Corinthian Yachtsman, or, Hints on Yachting, 1886

Daily routine: Make it rule with your crew be they many or few, when lying in harbour to be out of their hammocks at an early hour. Let the decks be washed down first thing, the grating scrubbed, the bulwarks washed, the copper scoured, brasses cleaned and polished, running gear overhauled and made hard taut; ropes all coiled away in their proper places, water and coke or other fuel got on board, hammocks and bedding stowed away, the forecastle scoured and cleaned out, and the galley fire lit, the boats washed out and overhauled, their oars, thole pins and crutches, rudders, yokes and lines, and respective boat hooks laid ready for use; these duties should be completed by 8 o-clock at which hour punctually you should display your burgee and ensign; afterwards the crew will cleanse themselves and get their breakfasts.

"VANDERDECKEN" [William Cooper]
The Yacht Sailor, 1862

Whoever wishes to make poor Jack have a happy life of it, will try to furnish him with a good sound bottom of religious faith and knowledge, whereon to build up all the rest of his mental cargo.

He should be able to read his bible well; and I would recommend that he should study the best book of practical morality that I know of – Robinson Crusoe; that takes of all others the most level to his comprehension, and the best suited to his daily life.

The Chaplain of the Royal Welsh Yacht Club
School for Sailors.
Hunt's Yachting Magazine, 1863

Every facility towards cleanliness and order of their persons and habits should be afforded, and thus having a place for everything provided, with all the requisites for their personal accommodation, there can be no excuse for slovenliness and neglect.

"VANDERDECKEN" [William Cooper]
Yachts and Yachting, 1873

Never permit your yacht to be disfigured by washed clothes hung to dry in improper places, such as on the bowsprit and shrouds etc. There should be regular days for washing, and clothes lines fitted, yacht sailors frequently delight to transgress these rules, and above all are remarkably fond of displaying shirts to dry on Sunday morning. Check such disgraceful exhibitions, nothing but continued bad weather at sea can palliate them.

Hints to Young Hands in Yachting Matters by a
Veteran Yachtsman
Hunt's Yachting Magazine, 1852

Clothes for the Summer Cruise

The bag of working clothes:

4 flannel shirts
2 pairs of flannel pygamas
$\frac{1}{2}$ doz. pairs of socks, 2 pairs
of which should be thick
2 pairs of thick warm
stockings
1 pair of warm slippers
2 pairs of common blue india
rubber soled shoes
1 pair of brown leather shoes
2 blue guernseys, hand knit

4 bath towels and $\frac{1}{2}$ dozen
others
Sleeping bag
Dressing case
1 suit of thick pilot cloth
1 old pair of thick blue
trousers
1 large thick square comforter
1 common serge suit
1 pair of mittens
1 pair of tanned leather boots

A tin case for shore going clothes (including the following):

A dress suit and shoes
A shore-going suit
3 linen shirts

6 collars
White ties
Gloves

For comfort in a small yacht it is impossible to do with less. Of course it may be thought foolish taking the tin case stocked as it is, but experience has taught that even in the wildest and most out-of-the-way spots, occasions arise when all pleasure is spoiled by not having the evening change of kit at hand.

G. L. BLAKE
5 Tonners and 5 Raters in the North.
Yachting. Vol. I; edited by His Grace the Duke of Beaufort,
1894

Nowadays in hot weather many yachtsmen wear next to nothing at all and I have even seen men prancing about on deck in their "birthday suits". This cult of the nude is being carried too far. Some time ago my wife and I were in a village shop and a man came in wearing nothing but shorts and canvas shoes. My wife was disgusted and remarked to me "If that is how yachtsmen dress, I don't think much of them".

FRANCIS B. COOKE
Cruising Hints, 1948

Take care that your apparel is suitable for the type of yacht to which you are going. "Yachting" clothes have a wide range, from a pair of grey flannel trousers (possibly darned), a shirt of doubtful hue, with a sweater of the same colour, to immaculate "ducks", a yachting cap and a clean collar for each day of the week (but in yachting the apparel does not necessarily 'oft proclaim' the sailor.)

L. F. CALLINGHAM
Jottings for the Young Sailor, 1943

The clothing (of paid hands) by the way is seldom worn out at the end of the summer and the man, knowing that he will get a new rig out the next season, sells it. We have frequently seen farm labourers and others in the neighbourhood of a yachting centre wearing guernseys bearing the names of famous yachts.

From the Man at the Wheel
Yachtsman and Motor Boating, 1934

An automobile robe or a steamer rug is grand protection to the helmsman on a cold day or night.

A night watchman often keeps warm with a couple of lanterns placed under the blanket wrapped around his legs. Try it some cold wet night at the helm.

HAROLD AUGUSTIN CALAHAN
Gadgets and Wrinkles, 1938

29

My means have never enabled me to attain to the dignity of possessing a large yacht, but I have a snug little yawl of eighty tons, which I find quite sufficient for channel cruising, although no doubt too small to afford much comfort if I wished to make longer trips.

My season afloat never exceeds twelve weeks and my weekly cost is £50.

I have no unusual expenses: I never have more than two friends with me. Indeed I have not room for any more unless I were to put two into a cabin.

My crew consists of nine. As I like to have things done smartly, the crew is none too large. At any rate I could only spare one seaman, or I should have no gig's crew, and the saving in money would only amount to about £30 (a year).

My cook has no sinecure, as he cooks for all hands, fore and aft, my steward has also plenty to do, and his duties comprehend what on shore would belong to butler, valet, and housemaid combined. On the whole I am pretty sure I keep "no more cats than catch mice".

Expenses of Keeping a Yacht.
Hunt's Yachting Magazine, 1885

Old sailor men

The older and more experienced the helmsman or seaman the more exactly does he observe it as a second nature, and they steer better than anybody off the wind on a reach in a heavy sea. Have you ever noticed the funny way these old fashioned fishermen sort of roll about, and when standing on deck they have a way of standing or balancing first on one leg and then on the other? This comes from "meeting her". It is very odd, but it is a fact! They are always in body and mind "meeting her", that is, they are meeting the motion of the vessel on the seas in precisely the same way they do with the helm as the vessel runs over the waves. You cannot, however, steer well in a heavy sea unless you have the habit of "meeting her", and it can only be found by practice. We hope the beginner will not think we are conjuring him to adopt a style of a "pantomime sailor".

B. HECKSTALL SMITH
Yacht Racing, 1923

Off Yarmouth – The 'Short Blue' Fleet

On Sunday morning, shortly after breakfast, we made out the fleet, with most of the vessels near us hove to, a steamer being among them, stationary, like the rest. In the distance were many other vessels, some standing towards the fleet, others sailing in different directions, and a few ships passing by. We found that several of them carried the 'Bethel' flag, a notice that service was to be held on board. Both yachts hove to and we pulled on board one of the vessels. We were gladly received by the master who was going to conduct the service. The crew of several other vessels having come on board, he invited us to join them, which we willingly did, although the space was somewhat confined. Several hymns were sung, the fine manly voices of the fishermen producing a good effect.

W. H. G. KINGSTON
A Yacht Voyage Round England, [1890]

Lifebelts: A very simple one. Keep all the beer and other corks which may be drawn in the house, and get a friend or two to do the same, until you have a sufficient number, then thread them lengthwise on stout spunyarn and weave an oblong mat with them, taking care that the intersections of the yarn come between the corks. A double web of these with strings at the ends to tie, or straps to buckle would do capitally. To make it look neater it might be covered with canvas and painted.

G. CHRISTOPHER DAVIES
Practical Boat Sailing for Amateurs, [1922?]

One of the most important appendages to a yacht large or small is the dinghy or as it was formely called the jolly boat. Without a boat of some sort it is not wise to get underweigh in even a five tonner.

TYRELL E BIDDLE
The Corinthian Yachtsman, or, Hints on Yachting, 1886

Nothing can contrast more with the majestic and beautiful appearance of a ship of war, and her fine seamanlike and otherwise well dressed ship's company, than to see numbers of her men going about the decks or on their various duties, without shoes. Much of this arises through not having a proper person on board to repair the seamen's shoes when requisite.

Capt. F. LIARDEL R.N.
Professional Recollections of Seamanship, Discipline etc., 1849

Accommodation for Ladies. The owner of a little 'pocket' cruiser may wish to take, say, his daughter or sister away with him but is debarred from doing so by a lack of cabin accommodation. This difficulty could be overcome by hanging a fore-and-aft curtain down the centre of the cabin, thus dividing it into two cubicles. In the morning he could dress in the cockpit, leaving the cabin to the lady. A cockpit tent would be desirable for use on wet days. If three or four cup-hooks were screwed into the cabin-top beams, the curtain could be put up or taken down in a moment.

FRANCIS B. COOKE
Cruising Hints, 1948

In the galley every movable item should be secured, so that even if the ship literally stands on its end it will not mean the end of your best dishes and glasses.

BRANDT AYMAR
The Complete Cruiser, 1946

Not long ago I shipped in a boat, it could accommodate two, and only two. She was new and so was her owner. A dealer in yacht equipment had loaded him up with six of everything like a young bride setting up in her new home. There were six tea towels, tastefully embroidered with the ship's name and the club burgee. There were six dinner plates and six soup plates and six small plates and six cups and saucers all of one pattern and decorated with the ship's name in gold letters and the club burgee in its proper colours. When we had stowed this lot, a set of saucepans and the washing up bowl and a six pint kettle and the shaving mug had to go on deck.

By the artless expedient of leaving the crockery locker door open and laying the ship broadside to the wash of the Dutch packet doing her usual 15 knots as she cleared the Guard buoy off Harwich I staged the smash of a lifetime. After that we went ashore to Woolworths and set him up afresh with two pint mugs – ex coronation and no saucers, two deepish plates and two small plates. The set of saucepans and six pint kettle went to a good home ashore. With all the will in the world you cannot set up a sort of floating caravanserai in a 5 tonner.

ALEC GLANVILLE
Elements of Yacht Sailing and Cruising, 1939

As for the man who brings a large suitcase with sharp edges and pointed corners aboard a small boat, it were better for him that it were hanged about his neck and he were cast into the sea, for the thing is unstowable.

ALEC GLANVILLE
Elements of Yacht Sailing and Cruising, 1939

For bedding, sheets are a bother, and the best way is to have a night suit of flannel, made after the fashion of the combination garment in vogue among the other sex. You can put a dressing gown on if you are still cold.

Of course, if people sleep on damp cushions, with a draught playing on them from a skylight, they may expect to sow the seeds of colds and rheumatism, or worse.

G. CHRISTOPHER DAVIES
Practical Boat Sailing for Amateurs, [1922?]

Be sure the stove is securely fastened. It is no fun to be chased around a cabin by a red hot stove.

Plumbing is a nuisance and a danger. A commode, of the variety used in the sick room, is an excellent substitute for the expensive, annoying, and dangerous ship's toilet and is vastly more sanitary than most ship's toilets. It must be well anchored in the boat, of course, kept empty and clean, and must be kept from spilling.

HAROLD AUGUSTIN CALAHAN
Gadgets and Wrinkles, 1938

The interior of a small yacht's cabin can be made to look very pretty and snug. The library shelf can be on the forward wall, with the aneroid on one side of it and clock on the other. On the side walls above the bunks the charts, guns, and fishing-rods can be slung. A rack for glasses and another for pipes can be fitted where more convenient.

As blankets that serve for the yachtsman's bedding cannot well be stowed out of sight in a small cabin, it is well to have them as ornamental as possible. Red blankets neatly folded up at one end of the blue flannel bunk cushions give a bright appearance to the cabin. The windows and the skylight should have little blinds – red silk looks very well.

E. F. KNIGHT
Sailing;
revised and brought up to date by J. Scott Hughes, 1938

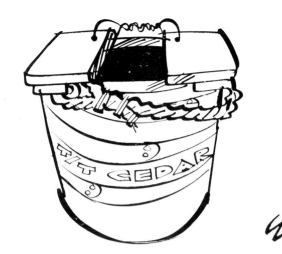

There are things other than physical comfort that are nice on a small cruiser, and one of them is the sense of complete relaxation that comes from being on a boat or vessel which has nothing that can explode and requires no fire than cannot instantly be put out with a draw bucket. The ear and nose should also be considered, and the cruiser which has no other noise than the water alongside and the wind in the rigging will give as much pleasure today as it did fifty years ago. However, on a perfectly calm, quiet night the regular tick of a perfectly poised clock like a Chelsea gives the cabin a very snug feeling while the varying gallop of the inferior timepiece is most annoying. As for the smells – if there is only a faint odor of oak, cedar and teak all will be well, for their combination will but enhance the ditty bag's fragrance of marline, beeswax and oakum while the fainter odors of sail cloth and manila add their soothing effect.

This is where the cedar bucket toilet comes in, for this arrangement can be used where desired and generally out of the cabin. It can be used in the cockpit at night or in the forepeak in the daytime. It has no everlasting odor, and for those who are affected by suggestion it may be kept hung under the after deck, when the whole ship can be as immaculate as a Greek temple. For those who have a rather tender posterior anatomy, the bucket can have an attachment to increase the areas of contact.

L. FRANCIS HERRESHOFF
The Compleat Cruiser, 1956

39

If most men are like the writer they are quite willing to sweep the cabin and cockpit floors but they detest the job of bending over and trying to sweep the pile of dirt into a dustpan, or worse yet, a piece of tin or paper. The broom is too large for the job and then, when you finally do get it all collected it blows off the dustpan again as you try to throw it overboard.

Perhaps it is a small matter, but there are enough annoyances without having this added. A sure end to the distasteful job is to cut a small hatch in the floor, have a shallow copper or galvanized steel pan made to fit the opening and of course a hatch to cover the opening. Now, when you use the broom, lift the hatch and sweep the mess into the pan and leave it there if you want until there is enough to make it worth while to lift the pan and gently deposit the contents over the leeward side.

The Rudder, 1925

Frequently raise the floorboards and see how much water there is in the bilge. If it is more than half way up the floor timbers pump or bale it out; otherwise a good list to a squall may shoot some of it into your bunk and bunks take a long time to get dry. Also it can smell. But the man who does not mind a wet bunk will not bother with details like smells.

S. J. HOUSLEY
Sailing Made Easy and Comfort in A Small Craft, 1930

Suggested quantities and commodities for four healthy persons setting out for a twenty-five day passage with sufficient for all emergencies:-

Fresh meat for 4 days say 16lbs.
Loaves of Bread for 4 days   12

A selection of the sea stock list:-

100 Eggs
30 lb of Flour
10 lb Jam
20 lb Onions
12 lb Butter (New Zealand)
49 lb Ships Biscuits
20 lb of Beef in Brine
17 lb Bacon packed in salt
10 large tins of condensed milk
 8 lb of Milk Powder
15 lb tinned meat
15 lb Carrots
 2 bottles Cocktail Cherries
 2 bundles of Cocktail sticks
 3 lb dried Prunes

15 large tins of Fruit
 2 gallons of Frying Oil
70 lb of Potatoes
 6 lb Rice
21 lb Sugar
10 lb tinned Sausages
 4 lb tinned Salmon
12 tins Sardines
 4 lb Suet
 4 lb Salt
 4 lb Tea
12 Cakes
10 tins Tomatoes
 6 lb Coffee
 3 lb Cocoa
etc. etc.

JOHN IRVING
Stores and Provisions
(John Irving and Douglas Service
The Yachtsman's Weekend Book), [1938]

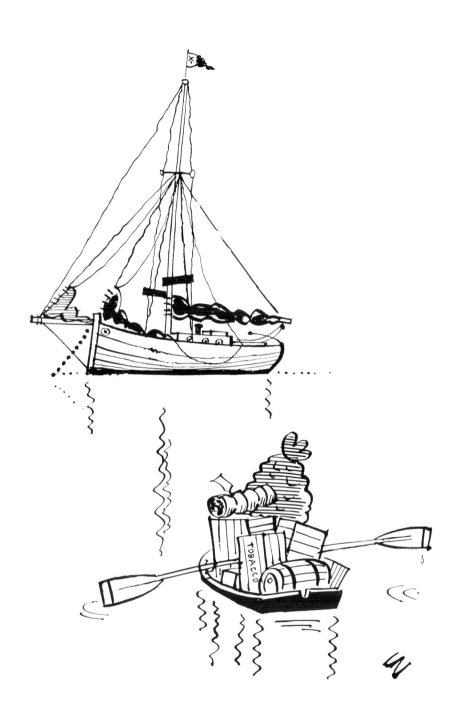

Porridge – Into the outer part of the double saucepan put enough river water to cover well the bottom of the inner part. Into the inner part put as many half pints of water from the jar as the you want porridge. Bring it to the boil. Sprinkle in the oatmeal. Keep stirring for 10 minutes. You may now reduce the flame and allow the pot to simmer for 20 minutes more. During this interval you may attack other jobs, tidying the cabin, or swabbing decks or completing your toilet. Put in the salt and then another 10 minutes simmering. Do not cook porridge overnight. It is best freshly made.

To summarize this most important operation:-

7.10 Light stove and put on pot.
7.20 Put in meal.
7.30 Meal thickens.
7.50 Put in salt.
8.00 Serve.

This is over a primus, a weaker stove may extend this by 15 minutes.

S. J. HOUSLEY
Sailing Made Easy and Comfort in A Small Craft, 1930

The eggs of marine birds may be found in great quantities on rocky islands about our shores, and many of them are excellent additions to the table when boiled hard.

Yachts and Yachting
Hunt's Yachting Magazine, 1864

We discovered that we were out of fresh food. I began to stir up a Christmas pudding. We had a few bottles of blueberry juice that my mother had put up for us, and by adding flour, our last two potatoes, some ship's biscuits and a little alcohol, it was completed. It was our one and only course that noon and, contrary to appearances, my mates claimed it was good.

AHTO WALTER and TOM OLSEN
Racing the Seas, 1935

On plenty of smart West Indian and other foreign sloops and schooners of about the size of our 50 tons, it is customary to do all the cooking on deck; and I do not see why this method should not be adopted on our small ocean going yacht when she is at sea in fine weather or lying at anchor. A tiny temporary galley or fireplace – very 'unyachty', it must be confessed – might be fitted up on deck forward, and if the cook be a West Indian negro of the right sort, he will probably be found as clever as an Indian 'bobbachee' on the march, at turning out a capital meal without the aid of a cumbersome stove or oven – and that, too without making any mess whatever, so that the skipper need feel no anxiety for his spotless deck and sails.

E. F. KNIGHT
Fitting Out a 50 tonner to Go Foreign
Yachting. Vol. I; edited by His Grace the Duke of Beaufort,
1894

Having a roast sirloin of beef, which had done duty at more than one meal and was getting somewhat ragged, Fred, who acted as chief cook, decided to make rissoles of the remainder. Coming on deck I was horrified to see him attacking the joint with an axe, what time he used the deck as a chopping-board. My shriek of horror arrested the blow that was threatening, and, bursting with righteous indignation, I poured the vials of my wrath upon him while I fondly examined my beloved deck.

PERCY WOODCOCK
A Cruise in Zoe
Yachting and Boating Monthly, 1910

Our feeding arrangements had by now largely broken down. One of the two hands normally cooked for us, but he was young, and it was considered inadvisable to wear him out by keeping him down below at the stove, which was forward, where the motion could very strongly be felt. The bread had given out, and all crockery was either soiled or broken. We therefore were reduced to eating bits hacked off a cold leg of mutton which we held on the settee, since the table had developed play fore and aft and nothing could be made to stay on it.

J. C. D. HARRINGTON
Driven Back: Windward's Stormy Cruise in the Irish Sea
Yachting Monthly and Motor Boating Magazine, 1933

For supper I got out the pickled salt beef; it was a grim story – part of the joint was alive with maggots. The other part looked all right, and slicing it up, I put it on to stew. The smell was rather strong, but perhaps only normal, and it tasted quite good.

COMMANDER R. D. GRAHAM
Rough Passage, 1936

A schooner skipper at home once showed me a tip for making the orthodox sea biscuit into a tasty dish. He steamed it till it was soft in the saucepan, and then fried it with the morning bacon, and it was very good. Up till then a sea biscuit had always seemed to me the form of diet least likely to tempt one to excess; indeed, I had only used them when ready, through absence of other food, to tackle anything. I usually ate them with the help of a coal hammer and at least a pint of tea.

WILSON H. ARMISTEAD
A June Cruise in Arctic Norway
Yachting Monthly and Marine Motor Magazine, 1915–16

Another cut and come again dish is boiled beef. Butchers usually have several pieces in pickle. Get silverside if possible. If it has been long in the brine the meat may need washing in fresh water or towing astern to remove the excess salt.

Major Gen. H. J. K. BAMFIELD and S. E. PALMER
Sailing, 1938

Boobies, bosun birds, frigate birds and man-o'war birds were nesting all about – some on the ground and others in low branches, and I was amazed at the ease with which they allowed themselves to be taken. Not a shot had to be fired, for all that we had to do was to pick the younger birds out of their nests. We did not take the chicks, but selected those which were almost ready to fly. Often, as we approached a young bird in its nest, it would disgorge the fish with which it had just been fed. Some threw up five or six fish, still whole and undigested, and these were readily gathered up and carried with us in plantain leaves. One booby disgorged eleven fish! I afterwards ate some of them, and they were delicious!

DWIGHT LONG
Sailing All Seas in the Idle Hour, 1938

Boiling – Cabbage – Cut into quarters boil quickly for about 40 minutes.

L. F. CALLINGHAM
Jottings for the Young Sailor, 1943

The healthful relish with which a plain hot breakfast of this sort is consumed with the fresh air all round, and the sun athwart the east, and the waves dancing while the boat sails merrily all the time is, enhanced by the pleasure of steering and buttering bread, and holding a hot egg and a teacup, all at once.

JOHN MACGREGOR
The Voyage Alone in the Yawl Rob Roy, 1868

Rub 'the worst' off the plates etc. with paper which you will throw
overboard. (Having an 'overboard' is one of the advantages of
living afloat.)

S. J. HOUSLEY
Sailing Made Easy and Comfort in A Small Craft, 1930

Fowling: Having a gun on board is no excuse for firing wantonly at every gull that flies near the boat. Remember that a rifle bullet skips along the water like a flat stone and any firing in the direction of other craft is dangerous especially if the rifle is a Lee Metford or other long range weapon.

"CLOVE HITCH" [Harry Robert], *editor*
A Handbook on Sailing, 1925

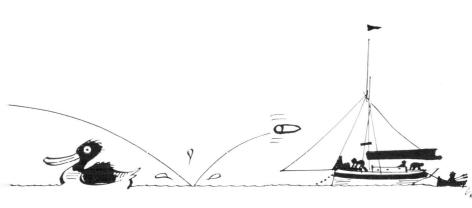

Cruising in foreign waters: Two or three days are quite sufficient to 'do' Bona and neighbourhood. Now whenever there is no English Church on shore, or if we are at sea, we always endeavour to have service on board, and this day was so quiet and fine, I arranged to have it on deck. All hands were therefore disposed decorously round the bulwarks aft, and I had got as far as the second Lesson for the day, when I became aware of sundry signs of inattention on the part of the congregation. This I would not notice till at last I myself observed a fine fat turtle fast asleep on the water, and which we were gradually approaching. I tried hard not to look at him, but it was no use and the nearer we got, the more inviting he looked, till thinking there could be no harm in securing a little fresh meat, I finished abruptly by giving the order for the dinghy to be lowered, which was eagerly obeyed, and our prey secured in a moment. I ought to mention, though, that service was resumed as soon as the boat was hoisted up.

Hunt's Yachting Magazine, 1870

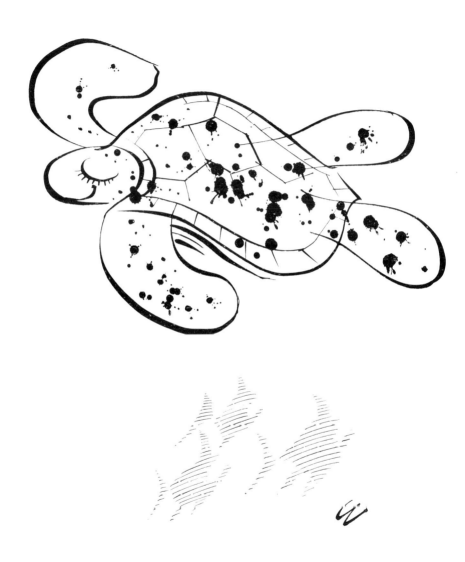

Man Aloft: Always steer with extra care when a man is aloft: his life may be in your hands, particularly if there is a danger of a gybe.

L. F. CALLINGHAM
Jottings for the Young Sailor, 1943

On my way back (down the Solent) I was nearly sunk by a shot from HMS Kite practising with a 30 ton gun. The shell burst between me and the target, and rained bits all round. I ran down to the gunboat and told them exactly what I thought of them and their shooting in the most varied language I knew.

LINTON HOPE
Boats I have Built, Patched and Tinkered
Yachting Monthly Magazine, 1898

Of seabirds, noble specimens are at all times within the reach of the yachtsman, gulls, terns, cormorants, gannets, guillemots, and puffins, he can pick and select ad infinitum swarming on the outlying islands.

A gannet decoy affords no little amusement when the birds are numerous and voracious for food; a piece of board, as near the colour of the sea as possible, should be veered astern for a considerable distance by means of a log line; upon this if a piece of cod liver or any small fish be fastened, the gannet will pitch from an almost incredible height upon it, and dislocate its neck in the concussion with the board, and will fall an easy prey; some noble specimens may be secured in this way without injuring the plumage by shot.

Yachts and Yachting
Hunt's Yachting Magazine, 1864

For those who wish to enjoy two summers without a winter, to see some of the most remarkable natural phenomena in the world, and the most interesting and most developed savage race with which Englishmen have come in contact; to explore fresh waters; to find an ample supply of good provisions, suited to European requirements; to live among fellow-countrymen who will as-suredly give a hearty and hospitable welcome, and to realise something of the extent, the variety and the vastness of the Queen's Empire, I can suggest no better nor more enjoyable cruise during the English winter months than one round the beautiful islands of Antipodean Britain.

THE EARL OF ONSLOW
Yachting in New Zealand
Yachting. Vol. II; edited by His Grace the Duke of Beaufort, 1894

Yarmouth I.O.W. It is the easiest port in England to get aground in on a rapidly falling tide, its apparent water is for the most part solid or any rate viscous, and its quay and bridge are always occupied by a selection of the local critics, from whose criticism few escape.

The berth I was supposed to occupy at Yarmouth was alongside a smartly painted vessel – a houseboat. Her owner was a sports-man who forgave me for scraping his topsides and always lent a hand. Only once did he get a little peeved when my bowsprit poked through one of his cabin ports.

J. A. WILLIAMSON
A Beginner in Sail, 1933

Another provision against the weather is a large umbrella for the use of any lady passenger when sailing under a strong sun. When in use the handle is fitted into a socket on the coaming of the hatchway, the socket being fitted with a universal joint, so that the umbrella may be adjusted in any desired position. There are two sockets, one on either side of the cockpit, in order that the umbrella may be carried on whichever side is most convenient.

JAMES McFERRAN
The Lady Hermione
Yachting. Vol. II; edited by His Grace the Duke of Beaufort, 1894
(*The Lady Hermione* was the property of Her Majesty's Ambassador at Paris His Excellency the Marquis of Dufferin and Ava.)

There is one thing we must suggest as a result of practical experience. It adds greatly to the enjoyment of the party if one of them brings his wife with him. A lady who is a good sailor and ready to put up with little discomforts is a great blessing. She is the softening, refining influence which puts everything straight, and of course, her domestic virtues are of the greatest assistance.

FRANK COWPER
Sailing Tours: The Coasts of Essex and Suffolk:
The Thames to Aldborough, 1892

One of the most important elements towards the smooth working
of the whole party is the presence of a lady, wife or mother or
daughter of a member; her advent has a humanizing influence on
the male members, however diverging their temperaments may
be. If she be an artist or a musician (every lady should be a
musician in its best sense) and does not object to smoking – if she
be an artist she won't – in a properly ventilated, not draughty,
cabin, her presence will be still more appreciated; and whether
she be ashore or afloat, the fact that a gentlewoman is a member of
the party helps to give a restful glamour to the whole cruise.
These remarks are intended to apply chiefly to small vessels.

G. L. BLAKE
Irish Clubs
Yachting. Vol. II; edited by His Grace the Duke of Beaufort,
1894

Sailing advice:
1. Never climb the mast of a small boat. If anything is wrong aloft, lower the mast and set it right.
2. Do not jibe in the middle of a squall, if you can avoid doing so.
3. If it is blowing hard, and all your crew are sitting to windward, remember that a sudden drop in the wind may cause the boat to capsize to windward. Unless your companions are experienced boatmen, do not carry so much sail as to necessitate their all sitting to windward.

E. F. KNIGHT
Sailing;
revised and brought up to date by J. Scott Hughes, 1938

'Mooring Snatchers': A friend went for a short sail and left his dinghy on his mooring. When he returned he found a strange yacht on his mooring and her crew had gone ashore in his dinghy. As an example of consummate impudence, that, I think, would take a deal of beating; but those who do such things are not sportsmen – they are not even gentlemen.

FRANCIS B. COOKE
Cruising Hints, 1948

If you have a novice on board who is going to pick up the buoy, tell him plainly to do so. We once had a man, quite a novice, on board, and upon his urgent representations, we allowed him to go forward and pick up the moorings. We actually hit the buoy with our stern: he looked at the buoy and waited; so did we in the cockpit; the boat began to gather stern way and we had to sail her again. He told us afterwards he was waiting to see her tie up to the buoy, as he thought something forward caught hold of the buoy. He didn't understand he was the something.

H. H. HEATHER
Sailing for Amateurs, 1910

It is surprising to see that you people have not taken up the motor launch. I don't think I have seen a dozen since getting here. The motor of today is a far different affair from what it was three years ago – aye even one year ago. When a man went to sea without oars in one of these boats he frequently had his family collect his life insurance before getting home, but today you can safely trust yourself and your family out in them. They are creating less trouble and profanity every year, and will soon be a boon and a blessing to men.

THOMAS FLEMING DAY
The Yachtsman, 1901

In cases when, to avoid collision, you must suddenly stop your boat by throwing your motor into reverse, you must sound three blasts on your whistle, indicating that your motor is going full astern and that you are trying your best to stop the headway of your ship.

BRANDT AYMAR
The Compete Cruiser, 1946

Advice to Amateur Crews and Guests.

Never go aboard a yacht except with soft rubber-soled shoes, otherwise damage may be done to the decks; and in any case, damage or no damage, you are likely to incur the owner's wrath and the next invitation may be long in coming.

Never talk to the man at the helm, particularly if racing or when special attention is needed.

When at sea don't make a habit of continual swearing; reserve it for special occasions.

Don't always want to be going ashore; you are presumed to have come for a yachting cruise, not for a walking tour.

L. F. CALLINGHAM
Jottings for the Young Sailor, 1943

East Coast Mud: If mud is too soft to be walked on, and mud pattens are unavailable, it is a good plan to sink down on the knees, keeping the weight slightly backwards; by this means the whole of the shin and the instep act as a large foot. Each knee should be slid forward alternately, and if the legs are bare from the knees downwards very good progress can be made over soft mud.

L. F. CALLINGHAM
Jottings for the Young Sailor, 1943

For coastwise cruising you need very few navigating instruments as you are seldom out of sight of land. A sextant is quite unnecessary when you can see the ladies bathing on the beach with the naked eye, and if you see such an instrument in a little yacht that spends her time in dodging round the coast from one river to the next in fine weather, you can safely attribute its presence to 'swank'. For cruising of this sort no extensive knowledge of navigation is required, and with the aid of a compass, lead and line, and the charts of the district you should be able to find your way without difficulty.

FRANCIS B. COOKE
Coastwise Cruising: From Erith to Lowestoft, 1929

Preparations for a hurricane: Cook two or three days provisions in advance. Register the barometer every half hour, see yourself all clear on 'the law of storms', lay your ship on the right tack and keep an eye to windward.

Lieut. A. H. ALSTON
Seamanship and Its Associated Duties in the Royal Navy, 1857

One great thing to remember when meeting steam vessels is they go much faster than from their size they appear to be going. Hence, it frequently happens that while you are tacking across the bows of a steamer, and think she will clear you by a hundred yards, she barely clears you by ten.

G. CHRISTOPHER DAVIES
Practical Boat Sailing for Amateurs, [1922?]

Notwithstanding all the rules with regard to power clearing sail, it is best in narrow waters to keep clear of the course of big steamships, even to the extent of losing some of the favour of the current.

If you are between two power vessels approaching each other end on and the vessels have barely room to manoeuvre, you will be perplexed as to whether to come about or carry on.

ARTHUR E. BULLEN AND GEOFFREY PROUT
Yachting: How to Sail and Manage a Small Modern Yacht, 1937

It is only the young navigator who never doubts his findings; the old never trusts any result until he has at least twice proven it.

From the Bermuda Race
The Rudder; edited by Thomas Fleming Day, 1909

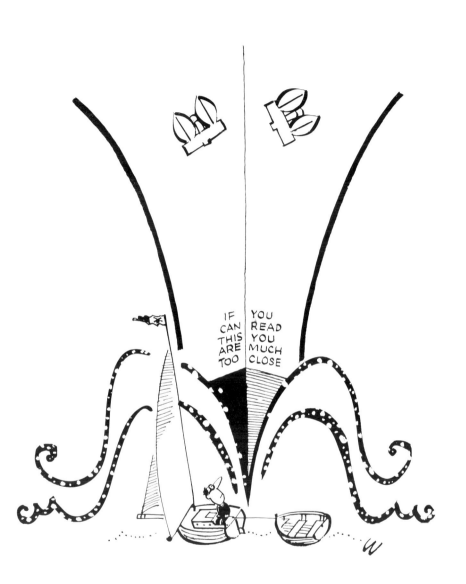

Yacht Clubs, like politicians and philosophers, are necessary evils which have been evolved by man in his desire to dominate his fellow-beings. No club which has ever been organised for the purpose of promoting a certain branch of sport sails under falser colors than do many of the yacht clubs which flourish in different parts of this old world.

The Rudder; edited by Thomas Fleming Day, 1909

When I received notification of my formal election, I attended at the clubhouse on a Saturday afternoon. I received a nod and a smile from the secretary and was introduced by him to the Commodore. This was almost like approaching the King, or what I imagine it is like to do so. "This is a racing club" said the Commodore "We race at three-thirty every Saturday and Sunday".

CLIFTON REYNOLDS
Sailing Small Waters, 1946

No doubt the single handed cruiser and small boat sailor of today, had he been born some two or three hundred years ago, would have been a pirate instead of a member of a respectable yacht club.

"CLOVE HITCH" [Harry Robert], *editor*
A Handbook of Sailing, 1925

Admiralty coast charts may be cut into sections of manageable size.

CLAUD WORTH
Yacht Cruising, 1921

Once a man, or woman, has discovered the spirit of racing in sailing-craft they will never give up of their own free will.

You can start racing today as a child, you can go on until you have to be lifted on board in your old age, and by so doing never realise what old age means.

Only a year ago I raced against a man of over eighty years who had to be lifted over the side of his boat, but was able to steer, in a breeze of wind, and after several hours win a prize. Such a man will be lifted on his horse when the yacht-racing season is over and enjoy a good day's hunting. Keen yachting folk never tire of the sport, and memories are worth recounting over again in the club-houses and on the fo'c'sle head.

S. HECKSTALL SMITH
The A.B.C. of Yacht Racing, 1935

It must not be thought that racing is the beginning and end of the sport. There are very many for whom actual racing holds no fascination but who prefer to potter about any old where that their fancy takes them in most weird craft without any turn of speed at all. Some there are whose sole joy seems to be to go round from one regatta to another and to end up looking like a Christmas tree with strings of winning flags hanging like rainbows. Each one to his choice, and far be it from anyone to detract from the value and enjoyment gained from competing with other craft.

Paymr. Lieut-Commander E. C. TALBOT-BOOTH
Yachts, Yachting and Sailing, 1938

The old time yachtsman would be at a loss to account for the delicate and complicated mechanism of the modern Cup racer, the deck winches, the battery of winches about the mast below deck, the main sheet winches and reels. The day of the watch tackle and the handy billy, luff upon luff has passed, and with it much of the real spirit and zest of yachting. It may even be that we shall see all manual labour replaced by electric winches and capstans, the helmsman having a battery of push buttons beside the wheel.

Yachting Monthly, 1920

The lordly yachtsman, resplendent in white and blue suitings and complete with golden cap-badge and co-respondent shoes, should never despise the men who race on every available week-end in salt-stained blue jerseys, shorts, bare legs, and maybe with jack-knives and marlinspikes hung round their waists. Such men are the backbone of racing, who merit our admiration and, although their boats may be only worth a few pounds, are probably better sailors than their more financially fortunate brethren who are taken off in smart motor-launches to their class racers, a few minutes before the race, to take hold of the tiller and answer obediently to the captain's instructions.

S. HECKSTALL SMITH
The A.B.C. of Yacht Racing, 1935

Acle Regatta

Twelve boats turned out for the start, and competition was keen. Those in front found themselves forced over the line, and some charged back into an almost solid mass of competitors. The scene of confusion, of minor collisions and of yachts locked together, was unparalleled in the whole history of the Yare and Bures.

CHARLES F. CARRODUS
Review of the Season's Racing Round the Broadland Regattas
Yachting Monthly and Marine Motor Magazine, 1925

One caution to the unwary. Some of the senior clubs are very proud of their ordnance, but racing boats of *modern* construction should give them a clear berth or the concussion may cause damage. One of the cracks had to proceed to the builders for repair soon after a race at which that great artillerist the hall porter of the Royal London yacht club shook Cowes to its foundations. Certain it is that some racing boats are now built far too light for safety if caught in a gale on the open sea.

"THALASSA"
Small Yacht Racing on the Solent
Yachting. Vol. I; edited by His Grace the Duke of Beaufort,
1894

The rules were not made to enable one competitor to bully another, but so that a number of boats may race together, often at very close quarters, with as little risk as may be. By this I do not mean that you should not "hit back" if someone tries to bully you. If, for instance, someone is trying to pass you to windward, do not hesitate to luff him good and hard, if you feel like it, and if he is so close that you hit him, let him go home. He will have no cause to complain. He tried to take advantage of you, and deserves to pay the penalty.

PERCY WOODCOCK
Small Yacht Racing, 1938

A yacht losing a man overboard must either recover the man on board before continuing the Race or give up the Race.

E. F. KNIGHT
Sailing;
revised and brought up to date by J. Scott Hughes, 1938

The habit of cheering a winning boat with three cheers, answered by three from the winner and then one more by the first boat, was a good old custom.

Another old custom on the bigger yachts is, or was, for the winning yachts approaching the finishing line to lower the staysail and jib topsail on the flash of the gun. If the yacht had a galley chimney, it was shipped and the cook stood by with a lump of waste soaked in paraffin, which he lit on the shout of "Gun!" so that a puff of smoke came up the chimney as the headsails came down. No doubt a hint of a well-earned tea!

S. HECKSTALL SMITH
The A.B.C. of Yacht Racing, 1935

The way some protests are justified would do no discredit to an Old Bailey practitioner.

The Corinthian Yachtsman, or, Hints on Yachting, 1886

With the best of intentions, men vested with a little brief authority as officers of the day frequently make the most ludicrous mistakes, and these mistakes are often not only countenanced, but confirmed by sailing committees anxious to uphold the decision of one of their number. Thus we have known an officer of the day dismiss a protest against the owner of a boat who, when on port tack, had wilfully forced another boat on starboard tack to go about for him and this in spite of the transaction having been witnessed by numerous credible witnesses. The matter having been referred to the sailing committee, the latter, to show their humorous tendencies, returned the laughable verdict of 'Not guilty, but don't do it again!'

The Yachtsman, 1894

Prickly Heat: Nothing is more discomforting on a voyage in the Tropics than the appearance of "prickly heat" with its soreness and tenderness, and its rash in quite the most inconvenient places. In the old East Indiaman days first-time visitors to the East were advised to sleep with a "Dutch wife" – a long bolster between their knees or under their elbows. If, in spite of such precaution, "prickly heat" still puts in an appearance gently dab the tender skin three or four times a day with a piece of soft cotton wool soaked in a solution of two teaspoonsful of carbolic acid to a pint of water. This should bring relief – and a "cure" in a very few days.

JOHN IRVING
Repairs to Crew and Ship
(John Irving and Douglas Service
The Yachtsman's Weekend Book), [1938]

Poisoning from tinned food, etc., indicates dosing with milk or raw eggs. Then make him sick – warm seawater as a drink will do this.

GEOFFREY PROUT
Brown's Pocket Book for Yachtsmen, 1930

A Brixham Trawler cure for seasickness is to eat hard ship's biscuits moistened with clean sea water.

L. F. CALLINGHAM
Jottings for the Young Sailor, 1943

If an arm or a leg should get broken, it should be set as best it can and the yacht put about for the nearest doctor. When setting a broken bone the secret is to get the limb to as near its normal shape as possible, and bind it in position onto a wooden splint. Anything will do as a splint, a piece of a bottom board from the dinghy, a strip of wood from one of the bunks, or anything of that nature. The essential point is to get the arm or leg straight and pulled out to its correct length before binding it up.

P. K. KEMP, Lt-Commander R. N. (Retd.)
Sailing, I: *Cruising*, 1938

Thunderstorms always give warning, and there is very little excuse for ever being caught unprepared. The best warnings are the weather reports. Look at the newspaper before starting out.

Even if you miss the broadcast weather reports, the radio is one of the best thunderstorm forecasters. If there is a great deal of static in the air, watch out for a thunderstorm. It is always well to listen for static for a few minutes before starting for a sail.

H. A. CALAHAN
Learning to Sail, 1932

Certainly the pleasure of a storm is getting into smooth water again.

Introduction by Sir Edward Sullivan
to *Yachting*. Vol. I; edited by His Grace the Duke of Beaufort,
1894

Laying up the toilet: All seacocks should be left open and all pipes should be carefully drained. It seems almost impossible, however, to get every last drop of water out of a toilet bowl and pump. Therefore, pump it as dry as possible and then pour a liberal amount of kerosene into the pump and owl, and pump enough to fill the pipe between the two. I prefer kerosene to alcohol as alcohol will evaporate pretty quickly.

Be sure to tie the lid of the seat down and put a sign on it "Danger – Filled with kerosene – Fire". Visitors to the boat in the winter (and there are hundreds of boat-crazy people crawling all over the boats in the yards every winter) may throw a lighted cigar butt into the bowl if you don't.

HAROLD AUGUSTIN CALAHAN
The Ship's Husband, 1937

The greater amount of physical work is undoubtedly performed by abstemious men. Above all activity and quickness are the main requisites.

FRANK COWPER
Sailing Tours: The Coasts of Essex and Suffolk:
The Thames to Aldborough, 1892

Just because your hair is sprinkled with the frost of the coming winter of your life is no reason for you to feel that the joys of youth have been snatched away by the ruthless hand of time. They can be brought back, but not unless you do your part. Sleepless nights, ravenous appetite, firm muscles and healthy tan, are all still at your beck and call. Nature still has them in her treasure chest and there is but one key that will fit the lock. A boat, as small a one as will fulfil your requirements is the answer to the problem of everlasting youth. Next Spring, next Summer, may be too late. Youth is at the door – call him in Now!

The Rudder, 1922

In all your dealings with the boatyard, remember the old adage that "the wheel that does the squeaking is the wheel that gets the grease". Try to do as little squeaking as possible but watch out for the other fellow who comes into the yard at the last minute and upsets all possible plans by squeaking louder than you do. He is often the fellow who runs up your bills by taking the workmen off your job while their time is charged to you. The only possible thing to do when you encounter such a "squeaker" is to "squeak" a little louder yourself. That is hard on the yard but necessary in self defence.

HAROLD AUGUSTIN CALAHAN
The Ship's Husband, 1937

An owner and friends arrived at the boatyard expecting the boat to have been launched. They find the boat exactly as she was when laid up six months before, plus the winter's accumulation of dirt and some one elses spars and blocks, which are arranged tastefully about the deck to dry after varnishing. Seeking the foreman, who is vainly trying to slink away behind the nearest shed, he asks in a voice of forced calm, but with a dangerous gleam in his eye, 'If they had received his letter ordering the boat to be fitted out?' only to be met by the unanswerable reply that 'we 'lowed as how you must 'ave forgot the tides were nips, and o'course us couldn't launch her till next springs'.

On waking next morning from sleep full of tantalising visions of fair winds and summer seas, they gaze in wonder at the large schooner which they could have sworn was hauled up beside their own humble cruiser when they were in the yard the previous afternoon, and which is now peacefully moored out in the stream.

As the yard is wrapped in Sabbath calm and carefully locked up, they cannot verify their suspicions, but return mournfully to town marvelling at tides that are high enough to float 200 ton schooners, but will not float 5 tonners.

LINTON HOPE
The Yachtsman, 1901

How many times when worried with business, or stifled by fogs, shall we see white cliffs, sparkling seas, dainty sails, and trim craft, grand headlands and sunny bays with marvellously gleaming sands, while the very thought brings whiffs of balmy air redolent of ozone and brimful of health. The deeds of the summer will be the delightful companions of the winter.

FRANK COWPER
Sailing Tours: Part II: The Nore to the Scilly Isles, 1893

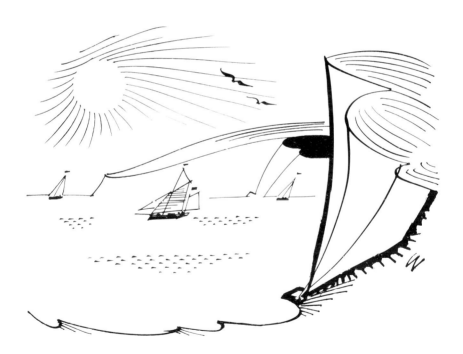

So we beat on, boats against the current, borne back ceaselessly into the past.

F. SCOTT FITZGERALD
The Great Gatsby, 1926

Bibliography

ALSTON, A. H. *Seamanship and its associated duties in the Royal Navy.* London, New York, 1857.

ARMISTEAD, Wilson H. A June cruise in arctic Norway. *in Yachting monthly and marine motor magazine*, 1915–1916.

AYMAR, Brandt *The Complete cruiser.* New York: Greenberg, 1946.

BAMFIELD, H. J. K., *and* PALMER, S. E. *Sailing.* London: Witherby, 1938.

BEAUFORT, Henry Charles Fitzroy Somerset, *8th Duke* (General editor: *Yachting.* 2v. London, 1894.)

BIDDLE, Tyrell E. *The Corinthian yachtsman; or, Hints on yachting.* London: Norie & Wilson, 1886.

BLAKE, G. L. Five tonners and five raters in the north. *in Yachting*, vol. I, 1894.

BLAKE, G. L. Irish clubs. *in Yachting*, vol. II, 1894.

BOSWELL, James *The Journal of a tour to the Hebrides.* London: Charles Dilly, 1786.

BULLEN, Arthur E., *and* PROUT, Geoffrey *Yachting: how to sail and manage a small modern yacht.* [2nd ed.] Glasgow: Brown, Son & Ferguson, 1937.

CALAHAN, H. A. *Learning to sail.* New York: Macmillan, 1932.

CALAHAN, H. A. *The Ship's husband.* New York: Macmillan, 1937.

CALAHAN, H. A. *Gadgets and wrinkles.* New York: Macmillan, 1938.

CALLINGHAM, L. F. *Jottings for the young sailor.* [3rd ed.] London: 'Arethusa' Training Ship, 1943.

CARRODUS, Charles F. Review of the season's racing round the Broadland regattas. *in Yachting monthly and marine motor magazine*, 1925.

'CLOVE HITCH', *pseud.* [i.e. ROBERT, Harry] *A Handbook on sailing.* London: The Bodley Head, 1925.

COOKE, Francis B. *Coastwise cruising, from Erith to Lowestoft.* London: Arnold, 1929.

COOKE, Francis B. *Cruising hints.* 6th ed. London: Arnold, 1948.

COOPER, William *see* 'VANDERDECKEN'

COWPER, Frank *Sailing tours. Part I: The Coasts of Essex and Suffolk . . . from the Thames to Aldborough.* London: Gill, 1892.

COWPER, Frank *Sailing tours. Part II: The Nore to the Scilly Isles.* London: Gill, 1893.

DAVIES, G. Christopher *Practical boat sailing for amateurs.* [3rd ed.?] London: Gill, [1922?]

DAY, Thomas Fleming (Editor: *The Rudder*)

DAY, Thomas Fleming *The Yachtsman*, 1901.

FITZGERALD, F. Scott *The Great Gatsby*. 1st English ed. London: Chatto & Windus, 1926.

GLANVILLE, Alec, *pseud*. [i.e. GRIEVE, Alexander Haig Granville] *Elements of yacht sailing and cruising*. London: Barrie and Jenkins, 1939.

GRAHAM, R. D. *Rough passage*. Edinburgh, London: Blackwood, 1936.

GRAHAM, Robert Douglas, *and* TEW, J. E. H. *A Manual for small yachts*. 2nd ed. London: Blackie, 1946.

HARRINGTON, J. C. D. Driven back: Windward's stormy cruise in the Irish Sea. *in Yachting monthly and motor boating magazine*, 1933.

HEATHER, H. H. *Sailing for amateurs*. London: Health & Strength Co. 1910.

HECKSTALL-SMITH, Brooke *Yacht racing*. London: Field Press, 1923.

HECKSTALL-SMITH, Smitheyt *The ABC of yacht racing*. London: Arnold, 1935.

HERRESHOFF, L. Francis *The Compleat cruiser*. 1956. Reprinted Sheridan House, 1984.

HOPE, Linton Boats I have built, patched and tinkered. *in Yachting monthly magazine*, 1898.

HOPE, Linton *The Yachtsman*, 1901.

HOUSLEY, S. J. *Sailing made easy, and comfort in a small craft*. London: Blakes, 1930.

HUGHES, J. Scott *see* KNIGHT, E. F.

IRVING, John, *and* SERVICE, Douglas *The Yachtsman's weekend book*. London: Seeley Service. [1938].

JOHNSON, Samuel *see* BOSWELL, James.

KEMP, P. K. *Sailing*. Vol. I: *Cruising*. London: Black, 1938.

KINGSTON, W. H. G. *A Yacht voyage round England*. New ed. London: Religious Tract Soc. [1890].

KNIGHT, E. F. Fitting out a fifty-tonner to go foreign: Baltic cruising. *in Yachting*, vol. I, 1894.

KNIGHT, E. F. *Sailing*; revised and brought up to date by J. Scott Hughes. London: Bell, 1938.

LIARDEL, F. *Professional recollections on seamanship, discipline etc*. Portsea: Woodward, 1849.

LONG, Dwight *Sailing all seas in the 'Idle Hour'*. London: Hodder & Stoughton, 1938.

McFERRAN, James The 'Lady Hermione'. *in Yachting*, vol. II, 1894.

MacGREGOR, John *The Voyage Alone In The Yawl 'Rob Roy'*. London: Sampson Low, 1898. (First published 1867; reprinted by Hart Davis 1954).

MINSHALL, Merlin Taking 'Hawke' across Europe. *in Yachting monthly and motor boating magazine*, 1936.

OLSEN, Tom *see* WALTER, Ahto, *and* OLSEN, Tom.

ONSLOW, William Hillier, *4th Earl* Yachting in New Zealand. *in Yachting*, vol. II, 1894.

PALMER, S. E. *see* BAMFIELD, H. J. K., *and* PALMER, S. E.

PROUT, Geoffrey *Brown's pocket book for yachtsmen*. Glasgow: Brown, Son & Ferguson, 1930.*see also* BULLEN, Arthur E., *and* PROUT, Geoffrey.

REYNOLDS, Clifton *Sailing small waters*. London: The Bodley Head, 1946.

ROBERT, Harry *see* 'CLOVE HITCH'

SERVICE, Douglas *see* IRVING, John, *and* SERVICE, Douglas

SULLIVAN, *Sir* Edward, *and others* Yachting. 2v. London: Longmans, Green, 1894. [Includes articles by G. L. Blake, E. F. Knight, James McFerran, Earl of Onslow, 'Thalassa'. General editor: 8th Duke of Beaufort]

TALBOT-BOOTH, E. C. *Yachts, yachting and sailing*. London: Sampson Low, Marston, 1938.

'TALLY HO'. *pseud* Completing your fitting out. *in Yachting monthly and marine motor magazine*, 1930.

TEW, J. E. H. *see* GRAHAM, R. D., *and* TEW, J. E. H.

'THALASSA', *pseud*. Small yacht racing on the Solent. *in Yachting*, Vol. I, 1894.

'VANDERDECKEN', *pseud*. [i.e. COOPER, William] The Yacht sailor. London: Hunt, 1862.

'VANDERDECKEN' *Yachts and yachting*. London: Hunt, 1873.

WALTER, Ahto, *and* OLSEN, Tom *Racing the seas*. London: Hurst & Blackett, 1935.

WILLIAMSON, J. A. *A Beginner in sail*. London: Arnold, 1933.

WOODCOCK, Percy A Cruise in 'Zoe'. *in Yachting and boating magazine*, 1910.

WOODCOCK, Percy *Small yacht racing*. London: Miles, 1938.

WOODCOCK, Percy *Fitting out*. London: Miles, 1938.

WORTH, Claud *Yacht cruising*. 2nd ed. London: Potter, 1921.

Hunt's yachting magazine. 1852, 1863, 1864, 1870, 1880, 1885.
The Yachtsman. 1894/95, 1901.
The Rudder. 1909, 1922, 1925.
Yachting and boating monthly. 1910.
Yachting monthly. 1898, 1920.
Yachting monthly and marine motor magazine. 1915/16, 1925, 1930.
Yachting monthly and motor boating magazine. 1933, 1936.
The Yachtsman and motor boating magazine. 1934.

S. J. Housley: Sailing made easy and comfort in a small craft. Published by Blakes Ltd., London, 1930.

Reprinted by permission of Blakes Holidays Ltd., Wroxham.

P. K. Kemp Lt-Commander R.N. (Retd.) Sailing: Part I. Cruising. Published by Adam and Charles Black, London, 1938.

Reprinted by permission of Mrs. C.C.F. Whitmell.

E. F. Knight: Sailing; revised and brought up to date by J. Scott Hughes. Published by G. Bell & Sons, 1938.

Reprinted by permission of Unwin Hyman, part of HarperCollins Publishers Ltd.

Geoffrey Prout: Brown's pocket book for yachtsmen. Published by Brown Son and Ferguson Ltd., Glasgow, 1930. Arthur E. Bullen and Geoffrey Prout: Yachting: how to sail and manage a small modern yacht. 2nd ed. Published by Brown Son and Ferguson Ltd., Glasgow. 1937.

Reprinted by permission of Mr. F. Prout and Mr. R. Prout.

J. A. Wiliamson: A beginner in sail. Published by Edward Arnold & Co., London, 1933.

Reprinted by permission of Mrs. Jean Easey.

Claud Worth: Yacht cruising 2nd ed. Published by J. D. Potter, London, 1921.

Reprinted by permission of Kelvin Hughes (incorporating J.D. Potter Ltd.)

The Yachting monthly. 1898 and 1920
The Yachting and boating monthly. 1910
Yachting monthly and marine motor magazine. 1915/16, 1925, 1930
Yachting monthly and motor boating magazine. 1933, 1936

Reprinted by permission of Yachting Monthly and IPC Magazines Ltd.

The Yachtsman. 1894, 1901
The Yachtsman and motor boating. 1934

Reprinted by permission of Practical Boat Owner and IPC Magazines Ltd.

We acknowledge Longman Group UK for use of Yachting. Vol. I. by Sir Edward Sullican et. al., and Yachting. Vol. II. by R.T. Pritchett et. al., in The Badminton Library. Published by Longmans & Green, 1894.

Whilst every effort has been made to secure permission, we may have failed in a few cases to trace the copyright holder. We apologize for any apparent negligence.

Index